HUMANISM

Barbara Smoker

1st edition   1973: Ward Lock Educational Co. Ltd
                     (reprinted 1976 and 1978)
2nd edition 1984: National Secular Society
3rd edition 1998: British Humanist Association
4th edition 2005: South Place Ethical Society
5th edition 2008: South Place Ethical Society

South Place Ethical Society founded in 1793 is the oldest organisation in the freethought movement. Open to all who share its values, the Society is an educational charity whose aim is the study and dissemination of ethical principles based on humanism, the cultivation of a rational and humane way of life, and the advancement of research and education in relevant fields.
(Reg. Charity no. 251396)

Published by:
South Place Ethical Society
Conway Hall Humanist Centre
25 Red Lion Square
London WC1R 4RL

Printed by:
J.G.Bryson (Printer)
156-162 High Road
East Finchley
London N2 9AS

Contents

Cover picture: *photograph from space of planet Earth, focus of humanism;*
with international humanist symbol

Dedicated to

inquiring minds,

of whatever age

Preface

$\mathcal{T}$HE word 'humanism' has more than one meaning. In its broadest sense, it is an attitude of mind that is centred on mankind and human interests — not to the exclusion of other animal species, but definitely to the exclusion of gods, angels, devils, and other make-believe beings. Generally, it implies a desire to think for yourself; to 'do your own thing'; to accept the results of free inquiry, whatever they may be; and to act in accordance with those results, in the light of reason, and in co-operation with others, for the promotion of human happiness.

When applied to the revival of classical learning at the Renaissance — roughly 1300-1550 CE (that is, Common Era, formerly called AD) the word 'humanism' stands for a passion for scholarship and the arts and a broadening of cultural horizons; but the Renaissance 'humanists' were still Christian. (Indeed, one of the best known of them, Thomas More, was canonised as a Roman Catholic martyr.) So they were not humanists in the sense in which the word is used in this book.

In the 20th century the word 'humanism' became a synonym for 'freethought', implying a rejection of religious beliefs based on alleged revelation. (No god; no life after death.) At least, that was what was almost universally understood by 'humanism' until the 1960s. Then the meaning began to be extended to include Christians and other believers who, while believing in supernatural life, were also very concerned with human welfare in this life. This has blurred the meaning of the word, so that some humanists now feel it necessary to call themselves 'secular humanist' or 'scientific humanist', in contrast to 'Christian humanist' or 'religious humanist'.

In this book the word 'humanism' means secular, scientific humanism — that is, a positive human-centred philosophy of life based on rationalism that is either atheist or agnostic, being concerned with life in this world, not with supposed gods or a hereafter.

5

However, the ideas of 'deists' may also be included in the compass of humanism. Although the two words 'theism' and 'deism' derive alike from the Greek and Latin words for 'god', they are used for different kinds of god belief: while a theist believes in a living, conscious, personal god with intelligence and will, the deist's god is an unrevealed, abstract creative principle without personal attributes.

Probably most people in Britain today live their day-to-day lives along humanistic lines, making their decisions according to experience and common sense; but those who also follow superstitions such as horoscopes, or who say prayers or believe in a future life, cannot be humanists.

The names of the philosophers and their philosophies are given in this book, not because it is necessary to remember them, but in case you want to find out more about them.

The 'happy human' is the symbol of humanism,
recognised around the world

Chapter One: The humanist tradition — its beginnings

*A*LMOST every child ever born into the world must have wondered, at some time or other, how the world began — if it did have a beginning. And how they themselves came to be in it — and how they came to *be* at all.

In the beginning

Learning that your parents conceived you only pushes the question back to how life began in the *first* place. Biologists are excitedly discovering the mechanics of it, but the fact that it actually happened at all is as amazing as ever. And the beginning of consciousness is more amazing still. (Without our highly developed consciousness we should not know we existed, or be able to wonder about it like this.)

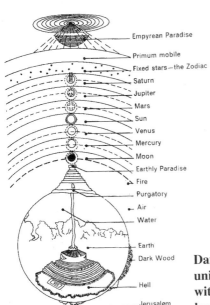

Empyrean Paradise
Primum mobile
Fixed stars—the Zodiac
Saturn
Jupiter
Mars
Sun
Venus
Mercury
Moon
Earthly Paradise
Fire
Purgatory
Air
Water
Earth
Dark Wood
Hell
Jerusalem

People naturally like to have answers to their questions, so they have been thinking of possible explanations for existence ever since they began to be human. The most satisfying of the explanations are handed down from parent to child, and what begins as guesswork is passed on as fact. In this way, each tribal community gradually builds up a whole body of myth to

Dante's medieval Christian idea of the universe, derived mainly from the Bible, with the after-life abodes geographically located (1300CE)

7

account for the world in which they find themselves.

One such explanation, constructed in Babylon about 2,500 years ago, appears in the first chapter of Genesis. It was such a satisfying story that it spread from country to country. Even today, with all the scientific knowledge we have regarding evolution, our solar system, and the vast universe beyond, some people still accept the biblical creation story as literally true.

Another basic thing that people wonder about is death. Life is so important to us that when we discover that all living things eventually die we want to be assured that it won't really happen to us nor to those we love. We are told (according to the religious tradition in which we are brought up) that we will go on living after death, through reincarnation, or through absorption into a 'world-soul', or through personal survival in another world. But is it true? (This will be considered in Chapter 3.)

There are always some people who, while living honourable and considerate lives, are sceptical about the faith into which they happened to be born — people who prefer to keep an open mind about the widely accepted explanations for which they see no evidence, or only evidence that is unconvincing. Thinking things out, they reject revelation. These people are in 'the humanist tradition'.

At some periods of history, humanism (under various names) has flourished as a respectable alternative to the prevailing creed; but whenever the religious authorities have been powerful and vengeful, those who questioned the orthodox creed have been punished and even put to death, so humanist ideas have had to go underground. But some sort of humanism has always been there, even if only in people's secret thoughts, as an alternative to religious faith. Can humanism be called a religion, then?

Well, it depends on what you mean by 'religion'. If you mean systems of supernatural belief and worship, then humanism is not a religion. But if you mean a philosophy that people live by, then it may be. I myself dislike calling humanism a religion, because it is confusing to do so. But a syllabus on world religions would be incomplete without something on humanism, since it is the permanent alternative to them all.

The ancient Greeks

The philosophical ideas in modern humanism have their source in the thinking of some of the ancient Greek philosophers, mainly congregating in the city of Athens, under its wise ruler Pericles, in the fifth century BCE. Athenian culture and democracy, which liberated the individual from the bonds of clan and family, have made Periclean Athens the model for what is called 'the open society' (which is a humanist ideal) to the present day; while its rival city, Sparta, represents 'the closed society' (the totalitarian regime). It is true that Pericles did not extend the rights of citizenship to slaves and women, but remember that in the USA slavery persisted until the 1860s and in Britain women did not get the vote until 1918.

In the previous century, two great atheistic philosophers had lived and taught in the Far East — Confucius in China, and Buddha in India. For 2,500 years their ideas have had a tremendous

Pottery picture showing Sophists in an Athenian school of the fifth century BCE, giving their pupils the individual attention that helped make it an age of intellectual brilliance

9

influence, and not only in their own countries, though the systems named after them have not always kept to their atheistic origins.

However, we must look to the philosophers of Periclean Athens for the chief philosophical influences in the western world, moulding all its important religions and philosophies.

Protagoras

One of the earliest of these philosophers, and one of the most important to humanist thinking, is Protagoras (484?-414?BCE) who founded the school of professional travelling teachers known as 'Sophists', on the principle that a little ordinary practical human knowledge is more useful than searching for the whole truth.

Protagoras taught that justice is a matter of agreed rules, not divine ordinance, and that 'man is the measure of all things'. In other words, that for human beings there is no standard, or ideal, outside human purposes and values derived from human experience and sensibility. This principle is central to modern humanism, and is in fact the main difference between humanism and religious faith. The religionist generally believes that human values derive from absolute values, originating in a god that is independent of mankind, beyond time and beyond this world. To the humanist, however, alleged divine revelation was actually thought up by clever men for the sake of greater authority. And so thought Protagoras, some 2400 years ago.

Although there were humanistic ideas around in ancient Egypt, as long before Protagoras as he was before us, Protagoras is sometimes called the first humanist. None of his writings (except a few odd sentences) have come down to us, but he is supposed to have written a book that began 'Of the gods I cannot say whether they exist or not'. This was probably a cautious way of saying he did not believe in them at all (for it was just as dangerous to profess atheism in those pagan times as it was in Christendom two thousand years later). Even so, there is a legend that he was forced to flee from Athens on an accusation of blasphemy.

Democritus, Socrates, Plato

Then there was Democritus. Perhaps he was a friend of Protagoras, as they came from the same city, Abdera. Democritus was a 'materialist' or 'monist' — that is, a philosopher who says that the universe is made up of matter (material things and their movements) — mind being a process of the material brain, not something different, and time and space being aspects of matter.

Instead of starting from the prevailing supernatural beliefs, Democritus studied nature at first hand. He worked out an atomic theory (first suggested by Leucippus of Miletus) that came remarkably close to the science of our own time — saying that the material universe comprised changeable combinations of atoms moving in a vacuum or void that had always existed. Democritus, who lived to be a very old man, was known as 'the laughing philosopher', because he used to laugh at the follies of mankind.

Democritus
(About 460 - 370 BCE)

Also living at that time was Hippocrates, 'the father of medicine'. He and his pupils freed their minds of religion — which not only provides answers without evidence but may even consider illness to be a part of the divine will. Hippocrates relied strictly on exact observations of symptoms — and some of his medical cases are described so accurately that doctors today are able to diagnose the diseases. This scientific care was matched by the humanitarian care that Hippocrates and his followers gave to their patients, whom they took fully into their confidence; and it added up to a humanistic view of medicine that has remained the ideal for doctors to this day.

Another very great philosopher living at the same time was Socrates (469-399 BCE). He wasn't good-looking, but the power and wit of his conversation could hold an audience spellbound. He used a method of discussion (called 'Socratic', though probably got from Protagoras) which pursued the truth by question and answer, 'wherever the argument might lead' — thus fulfilling the humanist requirement of free inquiry. Socrates said that the only way in which he was wiser than other men was that they thought they knew a lot whereas he knew how ignorant he was!

Socrates always insisted on terms being defined. That is to say, 'Before we start arguing, let us decide exactly what it is we are talking about.' In order to live good lives, he said, we must be clear about what goodness is. And he was never afraid to speak out for justice, even in unpopular causes.

As he grew old, Socrates had a big following among the young sons of the nobility. But, not surprisingly, quite a few people disliked him — especially the pompous ones whom he had made look foolish in argument. Besides, he was

Sculpture of Socrates (469-399 BCE), from whom all the great schools of philosophy claim descent

regarded as a threat to the established order. So he was accused of denying the gods of Athens and of corrupting the young. A jury of Athenian citizens found him guilty and sentenced him to death by a drink of hemlock. He could have saved himself by formally recanting his irreverent views, but he preferred to take the poison and die.

There is a graphic description of his death in a book written by one of his pupils, Plato (427?-347 BCE). In fact, most of what we know about Socrates (and, for that matter, several of the other philosophers of the day) is from Plato's *Dialogues*, for Socrates himself never wrote anything. He just liked talking. Plato wrote down a lot of the things he remembered Socrates saying, and, because the educationalists of later centuries favoured Plato, his works have survived.

Plato had a religious turn of mind, believing strongly in an ultimate reality behind the world we experience. This is the theory of 'Forms' (or 'Universals'), which he took over from Socrates and built up into a whole system of thought. These Forms are ideal prototypes — absolute, eternal and unchanging. They exist, said Plato, in some higher world, apart from their particular manifestations which we experience in the ordinary world, the manifestations being illusion, not reality. According to this Platonic philosophy, the human values of beauty, truth, and goodness come to us from the higher world.

This is a far cry from the down-to-earth theories of Protagoras and Democritus, and comes much closer to the Christian concepts of heaven (Plato's higher world of Forms), God (Plato's Form of the Good), and the immortal soul (Plato's Form of a person) than to humanist ideas. So Plato is an *opponent* of the humanist tradition, especially as he also advocated social hierarchy. Humanists follow Protagoras and Democritus, not Plato.

Aristotle

Just as Plato had been a pupil of Socrates, so Plato himself had a famous pupil — Aristotle (384-322 BCE). In his hands, the Platonic Forms became 'immanent' (that is, existent *within* natural objects) instead of being 'transcendent' (*beyond* them). Thus, instead of the ideal Form of an oak-tree existing on some other plane of reality, the Form is carried within the acorn itself as a *potential* oak.

Aristotle maintained that everything is caused. But to complete the chain of causality he decided that there must have been a first 'uncaused cause' and 'prime mover', to set the whole works going, for he found this easier to accept than the atomists' theory that matter had no beginning. He apparently failed to see that in supposing an uncaused cause he was contradicting his initial

13

assumption that *everything* is caused! Although he only meant it as a philosophical idea, not as a personal god, the Christian theologians of the Middle Ages seized on this Aristotelian theory as demonstrating the existence of God. They ignored the fact that Aristotle had also explicitly rejected the idea that mind or spirit could exist apart from matter, thus ruling out a personal god (or angels or ghosts) without a body.

Aristotle's teaching is called 'peripatetic' (Greek for 'walking about') because of his habit of strolling round the garden with his pupils while he taught them. His three greatest achievements, to a humanist, were: his inclusion in natural science of the study of man (mind as well as body), making human welfare the criterion of moral conduct, and affirming the great potential of humanity if freed from fear of the gods. But these important aspects of Aristotle's work were cast aside by the medieval Scholastics, because they did not fit in with Christian doctrine, and they were ignored until modern times.

While Plato had used methods of reasoning to try to understand the divine scheme of things, Aristotle used the same methods of reasoning to understand how things really were, and to put them to human use. These two different ways of using reason were the beginning of the cultural division between religion and science in Europe.

Epicurus

A year or so before Aristotle died, a remarkable young student, Epicurus (341-270 BCE), came to Athens from Samos. Unlike Aristotle, he accepted the atomists' theory that matter is made of everlasting atoms, so he did not need any 'uncaused cause'; and he explained the formation of the world by supposing chance collisions that set off later events, so he did not need any 'prime mover'. Epicurus held that there are millions of 'worlds' and that the gods lived in the empty spaces between them, taking no interest in human lives, so we need not bother about the gods. And he taught

14

a similar detachment towards life itself. He probably only brought the gods into it at all in order to avoid trouble: all that we know of his philosophy suggests that in fact he was an atheistic materialist.

A person's soul (or Form) was, he said, held together by the body, so the soul must die when the body dies. Death is simply the end of life, after which nothing can be experienced, and it is therefore unreasonable to be afraid of death. (One might reasonably fear a painful death, but nowadays that can usually be avoided.) In the next few centuries, a philosophical epitaph (in

Epicurus, a materialist philosopher who found everything explicable without supernatural causes, and taught that the purpose of life is pleasure

both senses of 'philosophical') appeared on the graves of many Epicureans (the followers of Epicurus) throughout Italy, Gaul, and Roman Africa: *I was not, I have been, I am not, I do not mind.*

What concerned Epicurus was the art of living. Taking as his starting-point Aristotle's principle that good conduct is that which promotes human happiness, Epicurus went on to define the good life as a life of pleasure and friendship, absence of pain, and peace of mind. His disciples included women and slaves, and all were treated as equals — an unheard-of thing!

It is a common mistake (deliberately fostered by some religious people) to picture Epicureans as greedily indulging in pleasures of the body. Epicurus himself lived a frugal life, providing for his guests some cakes and water, with a little wine and cheese at festivals. And he taught that peace of mind requires 'moderation in all things'. So much for St Augustine's smear that Epicurean materialism was 'a philosophy of swine'.

The chief rival ethical system to Epicureanism in the Hellenistic and Roman empires was that of the Stoics, who believed that men should not aim at pleasure, even in the moderate Epicurean way, but should try to make themselves independent of the pleasures of life. Although modern humanists are basically Epicurean, they approve of Stoic acceptance in a bad situation when nothing can be done to make it better, but not otherwise.

Epicurus is said to have written as many as three hundred books, but only fragments have survived. However, a famous Latin poem, *De Rerum Natura* ('Of the nature of things'), written more than two centuries later by a great Roman poet, Lucretius (99-55 BCE), popularised the Epicurean philosophy in its full application to nature and human life, and, despite its defiant atheistic materialism, somehow survived the Dark Ages. One line reads *Tantum religio potuit suadere malorum* ('To such wickedness can men be driven by religion'), and the poem (of which there are several good English translations) abounds in picturesque images.

One delightful Epicurean saying is *'Friendship goes dancing round the world proclaiming to us all to awake to the praises of a happy life.'* That is humanism, in a nutshell.

Chapter Two: The humanist tradition — its continuation

*D*URING the six hundred years following the break-up of the Roman empire there was so little education in Christian Europe that this period is known as the Dark Ages. Then, from the end of the tenth century CE there was a gradual revival of learning, mainly through Muslim Spain, for the Muslims had preserved some of the teaching of the ancient Greeks.

The thirteenth-century Christian 'Scholastics' set out to reconcile theology with philosophy. They believed that Christian doctrine could not possibly be against reason, and should be supported by reason. So they brought the Greek classics back into education. Little did they realise what a gamble this was.

The Renaissance

The revival of learning was very slow until, in the late fourteenth century, it blossomed into what is called the 'Renaissance' (meaning 'rebirth'). This was the transition period between the rigid formality of the Middle Ages and the enlightened freedom of modern times. The Renaissance 'humanists' (notably Erasmus and More) were not complete humanists in our sense, because they were still Christian. And the great artists of the Renaissance (like Leonardo and Michelangelo) still used religious subjects for their paintings and sculptures — but religious subjects with a very human look.

Later on, because love of the arts was thus associated with the word 'humanism', people who cared about art and literature to the exclusion of science began to call themselves 'humanists', though people in the true humanist tradition have always cared a great deal about science too. Indeed, the scientific method (that is, the method of observation, theory and experiment) is the humanist way of getting knowledge, as opposed to alleged religious revelation.

17

The scientific method

When scientists want to know whether they have come up with the right theory about something they do not look to sacred writings, they look carefully and honestly at the experimental data to see whether these support or disprove the theory. And if they disagree among themselves, they can discuss the evidence rationally, each side being willing to be proved wrong by the other.

The scientific method is the humanist way of finding out the way things are. Like scientists, humanists must be willing to change their ideas when these do not square with what actually happens. Followers of the various religions are much slower to change their ideas, for they generally believe that God has given them the truth and that everyone else is therefore at least partly wrong. Besides, religious people often seem to regard lack of evidence for their beliefs as a positive virtue, stimulating strong faith in 'mystery'. Not all scientists are humanists — but perhaps they ought to be, if people were always consistent, for science and humanism never accept conclusions as final, while it is characteristic of religion to do so.

The Measurers — a painting by Hendrik van Balen (1560-1632), showing people engaged in different kinds of measurement, with appropriate instruments, to symbolise the scientific method

The great historical breakthrough for science was when the new 'inductive' method of reasoning came into use at the end of the sixteenth century. ('Inductive' means forming general laws from particular instances that keep to a repetitive pattern and look as though they will go on like that forever; it is contrasted with the 'deductive' way of reasoning from general assumptions to particular instances.) Of course, induction was not really new, it had been the method of Democritus and Hippocrates two thousand years earlier. But after being lost for so long it was excitingly 'new' again, and it enabled men like Francis Bacon, Copernicus, Galileo, and Newton, to lay the foundations of modern natural science.

Scientific method has five stages: (1) making records of observations and experimental data; (2) induction — forming a general law which would enable such observations to be predicted; (3) deduction — predicting (from that law) consequences not yet observed; (4) testing such consequences by experiment and observation — trying to falsify rather than just verify them; and (5a) if any prediction turns out to be wrong, rejecting the law and going back to stage 2, formulating a new or modified law; or (5b) if the law survives critical tests, accepting it provisionally as correct until a future prediction turns out to be wrong.

The Enlightenment

The philosophers of this modern science, beginning with Thomas Hobbes (1588-1679) and John Locke (1632-1704), were called 'Empiricists', from the Greek word for 'experience'. All knowledge of reality, they said, comes from observational experience. Empiricism was a very important step towards modern humanism, though most of the seventeenth-century empiricists were still Christian. Those of them who denied Christian beliefs (such as John Toland) were persecuted and their books were burnt. But at that point in European history it was still confidently expected, as a matter of faith, that natural science would be able to confound atheism for ever.

Soon, however, it became clear that this confidence was unjustified, for, instead of supporting Christian doctrines, natural science came out more and more against them. One of the greatest philosophers of all time was a Scottish empiricist, David Hume (1711-1776), whose rational analysis of religious ideas left theologians in a hole — though many of them still try to wriggle out of it.

Voltaire (1694-1778) who, with his fellow *philosophes*, attacked orthodox religion and advocated social reform

A kindred philosophical movement called 'the Enlightenment' started in Paris with the great writer Voltaire and the encyclopedists Diderot and Baron d'Holbach. They and their followers are known by the French name *'philosophes'*. This movement spread throughout Europe, and beyond. The churches tried to stem the tide of disbelief, but in vain.

These eighteenth-century sceptics did not go so far as to call themselves atheists. For one thing, it would have been dangerous to do so; for another, science had not progressed enough yet to make it seem likely that there was no God of any kind. Most of them called themselves 'Deists', meaning believers in an unknown (probably finite and impersonal) supreme being. Other names they used were naturalists, rationalists, and freethinkers. (The last two labels are still used by humanists today.) But Christians usually called them 'atheists' or 'sceptics' or 'infidels' or 'heretics'.

In the British colony that was soon to become the United States of America, the famous inventor and statesman Benjamin Franklin was one of the several leaders of thought and action who became deists. Others included George Washington, Thomas Jefferson, James Madison and, later, Abraham Lincoln. In fact, the first six presidents of the USA rejected the Christian creed — which makes it ironic that today no one has a chance of being elected president of that nation unless he claims to be a 'born-again' Christian! The most outstanding of the English deists was Thomas Paine

The Mount Rushmore monument venerates four American presidents, three of whom (Washington, Jefferson, Lincoln) were non-Christian humanists, the fourth (Theodore Roosevelt) remaining tenaciously Christian

(1737-1809), a self-educated man who wrote three very important little books: *Common Sense*, which helped bring about the American War of Independence; *Rights of Man,* a defence of the French Revolution; and *The Age of Reason,* a devastating critique of the Bible (completed in a French jail when Paine was imprisoned for protesting about the unnecessary violence after the Revolution was won).

'It is the duty of man,' Paine said, 'to obtain all the knowledge he can and make the best use of it.' He influenced both the French and American constitutions, but Britain still lacks a written constitution — and Paine, to use a biblical phrase, 'is not without honour, save in his own country'.

The nineteenth century

One question that has exercised philosophers from the beginning is the question 'Why be good?' Religious people answer this by saying that man has to obey the wishes of a higher being. For humanists, though, there is no higher being to obey. So why should humanists be 'good'? This question will be considered in chapters 4 and 5; but here, in their historical place, the nineteenth-century utilitarians must be mentioned.

The return of unbelief in the eighteenth century, with no God to be obeyed or salvation to be gained, made the question of morality an important one. It was answered, at the beginning of the nineteenth century, by the philosophy of 'utilitarianism', put forward by Jeremy Bentham and James Mill and developed by Mill's son, John Stuart Mill, Herbert Spencer, Leslie Stephen, and others. The utilitarians said that moral law is based on utility — that is, based on the practical consequences of particular actions. And these consequences are to be judged in terms of

John Stuart Mill (1806-1873), a leading Victorian logician, political economist and feminist, and author of important books on ethics including *On Liberty* and *Utilitarianism*. Gladstone called him 'the Saint of Rationalism'!

human happiness. This was really a return to Epicurus, but the return had to be made in modern philosophy before humanism could be accepted as a moral system of thought.

Several new words for labelling people in the humanist tradition now came into use. In 1840 a courageous, self-educated freethinker, G J Holyoake, coined the words 'secularism' and 'secularist' (from a French word meaning 'worldly'), and these words are still used today. Secularists say that religion ought not to interfere with the law, education, and other ordinary worldly matters. In 1860, the word 'humanist' was used in print in our sense for the first time. Then, in 1869, the evolutionist T H Huxley coined the word 'Agnostic' (Greek for 'not knowable'). Some humanists call themselves agnostic (nowadays we are more sparing with capital letters), in preference to atheist (Greek for 'no god-beliefs') — though there is not much difference between saying that knowledge about any gods is impossible (agnosticism) and that one simply does not have any such knowledge and will therefore not assume that gods exist (atheism).

Today the more militant humanists tend to call themselves atheists, freethinkers or secularists, while those who are more ready to co-operate with religious people, and to avoid the subject of God in case it upsets them, tend to call themselves agnostics or humanists — but there is no hard-and-fast rule about it. Other names for humanists are 'rationalist' (from the Latin for 'reason' — reason, not revelation, being adopted as the basis of knowledge) and 'ethicist' (from the word 'ethical', relating to moral questions — the Ethical movement being concerned to establish natural grounds of morality); but these two meanings have rather gone out of use in Britain since World War II.

The twentieth century

In the first half of the twentieth century there were many outstanding humanists in science and public life, but perhaps the greatest of all was an English earl, who was a mathematician, a philosopher, a social reformer, and a political rebel. His name was Bertrand Russell. Not only did he bring together many of the philosophical ideas of the past and make them more realistic, not only did he add his own important contributions to mathematics and logic, but also he involved himself in education, in liberal politics, and in international affairs — for he did not think philosophers should cut themselves off from the practical issues of their day. What, he asked, would be the use of all his mathematical

23

The humanist philosopher Bertrand Russell (1872-1970) addressing an antiwar rally in Trafalgar Square in 1962

and philosophical work if the world were to be blown to bits in a nuclear war? So, although he was a very old man, and might well have allowed himself to ease-up, he travelled to conferences around the world, continued his writing, helped to launch the Campaign for Nuclear Disarmament (in 1958) and the Committee of 100 (in 1960), and took part in anti-war demonstrations in the streets. Thousands of young people rallied to his banner. It was like the story of Socrates over again, except that hemlock was fortunately now out of fashion! In his ninetieth year Russell was jailed, for the second time in his life, because, like Socrates, he was 'corrupting the young' and shaking 'the establishment', and he refused to promise to give up 'civil disobedience'. And from the age of sixteen, way back in 1888, he had been an atheist, a rationalist, a freethinker, a secularist, a humanist. He was also a strange personal link with the utilitarians, for his godfather was John Stuart Mill!

Between the two world wars, the British humanist movement had declined in membership, mainly due to apathy resulting from the decline of religion itself. But the Ethical Union was gradually built up again after the second world war, largely through the work of its Secretary, H J Blackham, who later became the first Secretary of the International Humanist and Ethical Union, which he helped to found in 1952, and the first Director of the British Humanist Association.

The humanist movement in Britain was also given a big boost in 1955 by the hysterically hostile reaction of some sections of the public and press when the BBC allowed the humanist viewpoint to be put, very moderately, by an Aberdeen lecturer in educational psychology, Margaret Knight, in a series of three radio broadcasts for parents. The extent and fury of the outcry seem almost unbelievable today. (Margaret Knight relates the story in her book *Morals Without Religion.)*

Rapid advances in science

Meanwhile, science had been making huge strides, explaining more and more about the natural world and so leaving less and less for supernatural explanations to get away with. The concepts of mass, energy, space and time were unified by the great physicist Albert Einstein (1870-1955) in a new theory of gravity more accurate than that of Isaac Newton.

Einstein - great scientist and great humanist

One of the most important biological discoveries of all time was made in England in 1953 by James Watson, Francis Crick and Maurice Wilkins, building on painstaking research by Rosalind Franklin. What they discovered was the structure of the DNA molecule, which enables hereditary characteristics to be passed on from parents to offspring.

As a development from that, a French biologist, Jacques Monod, made an exciting contribution to humanist philosophy with his book *Chance and Necessity,* published in France in 1970. (The English translation appeared in America in 1971 and in Britain in 1972.) Monod pointed out that everything that has ever lived, including the human species and each individual person, is the result of a long chain of accidents, caused by *chance* and

25

perpetuated by the *necessity* of chemical reactions, so could not possibly have any design or purpose behind them.

This means that there is really nothing left for a creator God to do. It also means that for every person, and every living thing, there were untold billions that might have been but never made it. Don't you feel overwhelmed at the colossal odds against your having come to life at all? The last of an infinite number of chance factors that gave you life was which of millions of spermatozoa happened to reach and fertilise which waiting egg. That meeting was what created the unique person, you. It is as though you won a huge dividend in a colossal lottery that had been accumulating for hundreds of millions of years.

Monod's evidence of chance happenings upset not only theists, clutching at a creator God, but also Marxists, who insisted that the worldwide spread of Communism was historically certain.

The title of Jacques Monod's book is a quotation from something that our old friend Democritus said, 2,400 years ago: *Everything existing in the universe is the fruit of chance and of necessity.* So Monod, bringing us up-to-date, also takes us right back to the start of our story of humanist thinking. But the ideas are no longer mere guesswork: they now have solid scientific facts behind them.

Animal evolution

In the middle of the nineteenth century, the English naturalist Charles Darwin, who devoted his life to careful fact-finding, collected a great deal of evidence pointing to biological evolution (that is, the theory that animals slowly change from one kind to another) through a process which he called 'natural selection'. Variations which help animals to survive are inherited as permanent adaptations and so lead to new species. This theory of evolution, which Darwin expounded in his book *Origin of Species* (1859), was strongly denounced by the churches as heresy, for Christian doctrine taught that the different species of animals, culminating in

26

man, had each come about by separate creation, as described in Genesis.

Then a younger scientist, Thomas Henry Huxley (grandfather of Julian Huxley), publicised the principle of evolution, specifically applying it to mankind. He was dubbed 'Darwin's Bulldog'. Darwin developed this theory in *The Descent of Man,* published in 1871. This made the clergymen and theologians more angry than ever. But exploration and research and the invention of better scientific instruments gradually produced more and more evidence for evolution, until most of the Church people gave in – at least to the extent of accepting a compromise theory, 'creation by evolution'. However, though a wonderful process, evolution hardly seems to square with belief in a compassionate creator, for it operates through the weak always going under.

A cartoon of 1872, ridiculing Charles Darwin's book *The Descent of Man,* by depicting the author as a monkey

Because the Judaic-Christian-Muslim religions traditionally taught that animals had been put on earth for human benefit, animals were generally treated inhumanely. Jeremy Bentham was the first philosopher to say that, in deciding how animals should be treated, the question we should ask is not whether an animal can reason or speak, but whether it can suffer.

In recent decades, biologists have shown the very close kinship between human beings and other ape species, whose emotions and behaviour – as shown in television documentaries – mirror our own. Some of the best of these TV programmes have been made and presented by the humanist David Attenborough, while another humanist, Richard Dawkins, has put these observations into a detailed scientific framework in his lectures and writings. His 1996 book *Climbing Mount Improbable* gives a very clear account of how natural selection works.

Richard Dawkins, a most renowned writer on evolution, and is a distinguished member of several humanist organisations

On the last page of his great biological work, *The Ancestor's Tale,* he makes this heartfelt statement: 'My objection to supernatural beliefs is precisely that they miserably fail to do justice to the sublime grandeur of the real world. They represent a narrowing down from reality, an impoverishment of what the real world has to offer.'

Creationism

Even though there is overwhelming evidence for evolution in the fossil record, there are some religious believers, called 'creationists', who still argue against it. Some creationists believe that Earth is no more than a few thousand years old, in line with the Genesis story, allowing far too short a time for evolution. Other more sophisticated creationists accept the scientific estimate of some 4.6 billion years (based on astronomy and geology, as well as biology) but postulate a creative purpose called Intelligent Design (ID) – that is, God in disguise.

One of their most frequent arguments is that something as complex as the human eye could not possibly have come about by sheer random chance, any more than a whirlwind could sweep up a pile of scrap metal and turn it into a functional car. But no one suggests that an eye could evolve by sheer chance – each small useful change is saved, as with a ratchet, through succeeding generations; other changes dying out. Complex eyes have evolved independently in the animal kingdom at least forty times.

When a dog-breeder, say, deliberately takes advantage of particular mutations to breed a new kind of dog — which may be very different in size and shape from the wolf, which is the ancestor of all dogs – the process is artificial selection. Except for being much quicker, it is the same process as natural selection, with the role of the breeder taken by the particular environment. It is also known as 'the survival of the fittest'.

The phrase 'the theory of evolution' is often misunderstood – sometimes deliberately, by creationists – to imply an unsubstantiated guess. But scientists use the word 'theory' for the best and simplest possible explanation fitting the available facts. A theory is no longer a mere hypothesis or guesswork. There is no *scientific* alternative to the theory of evolution, which, moreover, links in with the DNA code, common to all life forms.

A summary of humanism

Humanism is not a set of doctrines, but an attitude to life. To the humanist, the miracle is here and now. It is the miracle of nature: there is nothing supernatural about it. Because the humanist believes that this life is the only life we can expect to have, it is especially important to make this life a good one. So, although humanism is based on *atheism* or *agnosticism*, it is far more than that negative basis. It also includes positive commitments to make the best possible use of our lives – both for our own sake, and to help others. Humanists are concerned to make the world a better place to live in, not only for people alive today, but for future generations too – especially as the lives of their descendants represent the only sort of immortality that humanists believe in.

Above all, humanists regard each individual person as an end in himself or herself, never as a means to achieve something, however desirable that may be. In order to be a secular humanist one has to be an atheist or agnostic; but it is possible to be an atheist or agnostic without being a humanist. (The Russian dictator, Stalin, was an atheist, but he was certainly not a humanist, because he did not respect the human rights of people who disagreed with him.)

Humanists are also *rationalists*, because they regard human reason as the best guide we have in facing life's problems; but they are more than rationalist, because they take into consideration the whole of human nature (desires, interests, sympathies, imagination, emotions), not just the intellect. In their social outlook, humanists are *secularist,* because they want to free society from the stranglehold that religious beliefs still have on it – whether collective worship in British schools or preserving sacred cows in Hindu India while human babies starve.

Humanists are *freethinkers,* because they never hand over their minds irrevocably to any Church or Party, but remain free to think for themselves. Humanists use the scientific method, not only to explain nature, but in every aspect of life, and, as Bernard Shaw put it, 'never accept anything reverently without asking it a great many very searching questions'. Humanists are *materialists* – having no belief in spirits (mind without body). Humanists are *empiricist* in their approach to knowledge; *utilitarian* in morality; *Epicurean* in the art of living.

Humanists say that every responsible human being should be free to make his or her own choices and live in their own life-style, as long as they do not violate the freedom of others. It would be impossible for humanists to force humanism on other people or to persecute non-humanists, for if they did they would no longer be humanist. Humanism stands for the open mind in the open society.

Unlike Christians, humanists see no virtue in faith, blind obedience, meekness, unworldliness, chastity, or pointless self-denial. The humanist virtues are: a regard for what is true, personal responsibility, tolerance, consideration, breadth of sympathy, public spirit, co-operative endeavour, and a concern for the future.

Chapter Three: Reality – true and false

$\mathcal{W}$HAT I mean by 'true' is the ordinary meaning of the word - that is, *factually* true, to the best of our knowledge.

Young people often ask their teachers 'Is it true?' - and so they should. If it concerns something geographical or mathematical, the answer can usually be a definite Yes or No, whereas something historical or scientific needs an answer based on probability, according to the known evidence. But what if it concerns religious beliefs?

So as not to offend students who hold different sets of doctrines, teachers often get round the question by answering 'It is true for some people.' But that is surely a misuse of the word 'true': except in poetry, truth does not depend on anyone's belief, or on how many people hold that belief. The best non-committal answer would be 'Some people think it is true; others don't.'

Justifying non-belief

If humanism is a positive outlook in its own right, why do humanists feel they have to offer reasons for their non-belief in gods or a future life? Why use the negative word 'atheist' any more than, say, 'a-fairyist' or 'a-Santa-Clausist'? (Indeed, some atheists reject the word atheist because they think it gives the god-idea too much importance.) Why did Bertrand Russell, in 1927, take time off from his positive contributions to knowledge to write a popular

31

essay called *Why I am not a Christian* for the National Secular Society? And why, in the present book, are the humanist viewpoint and way of life not simply described, without any mention of other views?

The answer is that, historically, non-believers have been a small (and often persecuted) minority in our European culture, and those who think differently from the majority on any important matter are often expected to explain why they do not conform to the general opinion. Before long it will probably be the believers in God and Heaven who find themselves in the position of being asked to justify their belief. But not yet – not generally, anyway. Most people in Britain still have at least a vague belief in a personal god and the afterlife, even though only a minority have a strong enough belief to do much about it. So the atheist is still expected to justify his atheism.

God and Santa Claus

Adults are not expected to mention that they do not believe in Santa Claus, let alone explain why. But young children who, because of their age, are assumed to have this belief, often find themselves in the position of saying, 'I don't believe in him'. Other children of their age (or even, sometimes, teasing adults) may then challenge them about their denial of Santa Claus. ('Where do you think all the toys

Barbara Smoker

The great freethinker, dramatist and writer, Bernard Shaw (1856-1950), pictured as a bad-tempered Santa Claus because he disliked the wastefulness and commercialism of Christmas. One year he sent out a card with the words, 'Courage, friends! We all loathe Christmas; but it comes only once a year and is soon over.'

came from that he left at the bottom of your bed at Christmas?') In the same way, theists often ask atheists, 'How do you think the universe came about, then, if there was no god to make it?'

Not all theists assume that the existence of matter, forming complex organisms, demonstrates the existence of a creator – and few modern theologians would claim this – but most ordinary people still think so, as St Paul did nineteen centuries ago: 'For the invisible things of him, from the creation of the world are clearly seen' (Romans I). This way of thinking is called 'natural theology'.

Just as very young children think that Santa Claus is a sufficient and necessary explanation for the toys, so unsophisticated god-believers think that a personal creator is a sufficient and necessary explanation for the universe. But as children begin to grow up, they come to realise that the Santa Claus theory raises more difficult problems than the one it purports to solve. And so does the creation theory, though most people never really subject it to critical thought. If they did, they would realise that the idea of a supreme intelligence (without a brain), existing for all eternity, suddenly creating everything else out of nothing, and then keeping a fatherly interest in it all (or at least in one particular little planet), is on the same childish level as the idea of Santa Claus making and distributing all the Christmas toys.

But this analogy holds good only so far. Someone does act as Santa Claus and bring the toys, and it is reasonable to seek explanations for such happenings. What we mean by explanations, though, is finding causal relationships between one event and another. When considering the whole universe, as a totality and throughout eternity, it is meaningless to ask for an explanation since there is (by definition) nothing else to relate it to. So god-believers place God outside the universe, as its explanation. But then: what explains God? As the 9th century CE Indian poet wrote:

Some foolish men declare that a Creator made the world. The doctrine that the world was created is ill-advised and should be rejected. (Quoted in *Some Ancestors of Humanism* by Leslie Scrase.)

Existence

God, it is said, is the answer to the question 'Why does anything exist at all?' But if it is necessary to explain existence, you would still have to explain why and how God existed. So the god-idea doesn't provide a final answer, unless you then assert that God existed from all eternity, uncaused. And why should that be any easier to accept than that matter/energy existed from all eternity, uncaused?

Existence seems such a miraculous thing, it is little wonder that there have been supernatural ideas to account for it from the time that human beings first became capable of abstract thought, nor that such ideas are still widely accepted. But is it reasonable to look for an explanation of existence? There are only two possibilities – either something existing or nothing existing – and the plain fact is that things do exist. You cannot go further back than existence, for there is no prior context of non-existence in which to place it.

However, it certainly *seems* amazing to us, who are part of it and conscious of it. The mind-boggling vastness of the universe (in relation to human size), its timescale, and its incomprehensible complexity, all add to the wonder of it – though the complexity is possible just because of the vastness and the timescale.

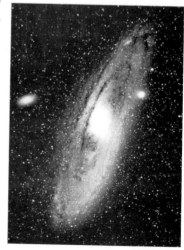

For the past four centuries scientists have been discovering how facets of the universe work and how organisms evolve, and, as new evidence emerges, theories previously held become untenable, and new models are proposed that fit the facts better. The whole joy of science is that it is not just a once-for-all revelation but a cumulative human

The Great Spiral Nebula in Andromeda, which can just be seen with the naked eye

34

endeavour, continually answering further questions posed by past research. The science of cosmology, especially, is at present in a stage of rapid development, and we are tentatively piecing together the cosmic jigsaw puzzle. Recent discoveries favour the 'Big Bang' theory for the origin of our universe. But that does not mean it came out of nothing. More likely, as one theory describes, the universe 'oscillates' – expanding and collapsing alternately, without any beginning, without any end.

According to supporters of this theory, the universe is likely to go on expanding for billions of years yet, but eventually it may begin to slow down. This means we can expect the whole process to go into reverse. Everything in the universe will then rush together, faster and faster, to form the densest possible mass once more.

In this way, the universe would pulsate in a periodic manner between very dense and very distended states – each approximately symmetric cycle beginning with a 'Big Bang' and ending with a 'Big Crunch'. However, some cosmologists think that the universe will just go on expanding for ever.

At some point during galactic evolution, a planet here and there happens to have the right physical and chemical conditions to produce living things, and some of the living things eventually may evolve consciousness.

Infinity

It is far easier to accept as probable the eternity of ever-changing matter and energy (as Democritus suggested nearly five hundred years before the Christian era), than the alternative theory that matter suddenly came into existence at some point in time, before which there was nothing – or nothing except an all-powerful spirit with a sudden creative urge.

Many religious people say that taking a scientific view of the universe must destroy our sense of awe and wonder, which they often call 'spirituality' or 'the religious emotion'. But this emotion,

35

which is certainly not dependent upon religious beliefs, comes from thinking about the observable universe. To suggest that trying to understand things scientifically might undermine the magic is like warning people against studying the techniques of Beethoven and Rembrandt lest seeing how they achieved their effects might destroy one's appreciation of their genius. Surely the contrary is the case.

Most educated people today, including theologians, agree with the scientific humanist view that matter/energy has always existed and that life came about through chemical reactions and evolved through mutation and natural selection. Modern theologians often protest when arguments like the above are put, knocking down natural theology – because, they say, Christian faith does not depend on natural theology. This may well be true of their own individual faith, but it is not true of the faith of most Christians. Schoolchildren are still taught natural theology at school; their teachers probably accept it; and so do many clergy. Even those clergy who have discarded natural theology for themselves continue to encourage the belief in their congregations – or, at least, say nothing openly to discourage it. But in their scholarly books and lectures theologians say that people need a religious faith not in order to provide supernatural explanations for the natural world but in order to give meaning to their lives.

Different religions occur mainly in particular countries because children generally keep to the religion of their parents

Major belief systems of the world

The argument seems to be that human beings need a superhuman being to look up to, and a life beyond death to look forward to. Whether these are human needs or not, the question still remains as to whether they are actually *true*. But in any case, would a person's life really have no value or purpose unless it were immortal? As Bertrand Russell said, 'Happiness is none the less true happiness because it must come to an end, nor do thought and love lose their value because they are not everlasting.'

Individual purposes

Humanists do not believe in cosmic values or ultimate purpose, but they do believe in earthly values and in the individual purposes which we give to our own lives as we live them. After all, people go on holiday, even though they know it is just for a week or two. They don't say, 'We'll only have to come home again at the end of the holiday, so there is no point in going.' In the same way, life can be worthwhile even though transitory.

Maybe it *would* help to make our lives more satisfactory if there really were an almighty God taking a personal interest in us and we

37

really were going to live for ever in a perfect world. But humanists prefer not to kid themselves with wishful thinking. Admittedly, it often takes courage to face reality and live without the drug of religious belief, but humanists try to cultivate that courage in themselves. They accept life on its own terms – with all its troubles and uncertainties, and with its one final certainty of death – while doing their best to make things better. For it is all the more pressing to do something about unhappiness here and now if you do not believe in a loving god who will see to it that everything turns out right in the end.

Death

Death is generally regarded as an evil – even by people who believe in heaven. But death is essential to life. Without death there could be no birth, no evolution, no younger generations coming along, and certainly no chance of promotion! 'We should not,' said Herbert Samuel, 'see death as an injury, but rather life as a privilege.'

To the humanist, death is simply, as Epicurus said, the end of life. To most religious people, however, it is a transition to a better life. Indeed, it is fair to say that the doctrine of a life hereafter is the one ingredient that makes religion so popular. But this is what Bernard Shaw said about it: 'Now the man who has come to believe that there is no such thing as death, the change so called being merely the transition to an exquisitely happy and utterly careless life, has not overcome the fear of death at all: on the contrary, it has overcome him so completely that he refuses to die on any terms whatever.'

I have noticed that whenever I question the existence of God, one reply I get is that this world is so wonderful it must have been designed by a supreme being; but when I question the belief in an afterlife, this world is said to be so bad that there must be another one ready to put it right! Since life on earth is so unjust, it is argued that there must be another life to redress the balance. But why
38

should injustice here lead to an expectation of justice elsewhere?

Anyway, why are most people so desirous of an afterlife? They generally think of it as life in a perfect world. But a perfect world would necessarily be static – and, surely, very boring!

The chief motive for belief in an afterlife is the unhappiness of being separated from those who are dear to us, particularly when the separation is the permanent one of death. But friends who meet in this life after a lapse of, say, twenty years find that they no longer really know one another. Besides, living on hope is not really living; it is only marking time. To live, you have to build new personal relationships. And even if the belief in reunion gives people comfort, this is no guarantee of its truth.

The chief *theological* argument for an afterlife is that the existence of an omnipotent God of love demands it. But this world, on the religious theory, is as much God's design as any other, and if he cannot or will not prevent evil from triumphing here, why assume he can or will manage things better elsewhere? Anyway, the argument is pointless except for those who already have an unshakable belief in a God of love and justice.

But is personal survival after death a *possibility?* This raises the whole question of personal identity. What could survive that would still really be *you?* Your identity depends on your memories, your likes and dislikes, and all your funny little ways. These depend on a living brain, on your particular biochemistry, where you live, the way in which you have been educated, and the way life treats you. And, of course, your personality, your opinions, your appearance, and your body cells all change very much during life. Supposing you were to go to heaven exactly as you were the day you were born, or as you may become by the end of a long life, would you regard that new- born baby or that senile centenarian as being really *you?* If you decide that it is the genetic potential that is the real you, what about identical twins? Are they really only one person? The more you think about it, the more snags you will see.

Religious experience

Some of the psychological conditions called 'religious experiences' are fairly common, and very real to the people they happen to. They are sometimes triggered off by religious meditation, but may also be caused by certain drugs, or by music, or by nothing obvious at all. They are a form of ecstasy, and may be related to sexual emotion. The feeling is sometimes described as one of being absorbed into the cosmos. A single experience can have a lifelong effect on the person's behaviour, especially if he or she believes that it had a supernatural origin. Sudden conversions are often of this nature – but the conversions are to various faiths, so can hardly indicate reliable divine communication.

People *want* to believe in so-called psychic phenomena — particularly ghosts – so that they can contact their dead friends and relations, and as evidence that they themselves will not really die. They want to believe in heaven. They want to believe in an all-powerful God who loves them and will look after them. And so they believe. Some subscribe to incompatible sets of belief at the same time – for instance, Christianity and reincarnation!

If they derive comfort from their beliefs, is it not wrong to disturb their faith? It would certainly be wrong to take away the religious consolation of anyone who was bereaved or ill or old or dying. But people in normal health are a different matter. Besides, humanists don't force their opinions on other people, as some religionists do; they just say what they really think when the occasion arises. But they do think it important to uphold the truth rather than just what is comforting or advantageous.

Anyway, religious beliefs are by no means always a comfort. They can be frightening. And even comfort may not always be a good thing: Karl Marx called religion 'the opium of the people' because it made them content with their lot instead of demanding better conditions. That is why the ruling class has always been in favour of religion. And why, even today, the churches don't have to pay rates and taxes like other organisations. And one reason why there is so much religion in schools and on the radio and television.

Religion in schools

" By the way, Grindley, I take it you're aware of your right to opt out of the daily act of worship?"

A cartoon from *Punch* showing an unlikely school assembly situation

Humanists think it is wrong to indoctrinate children in a particular set of beliefs, especially in a country where beliefs differ as much as they do in Britain today.

In some countries, such as the USA, it is against the law to introduce religion into schools, but in Britain it is actually against the law *not* to introduce it! Under the Education Acts, every state school is bound to provide religious education and to hold a daily collective act of worship – as though Parliament were competent to guarantee the existence of something or someone that should be worshipped. The law allows parents to withdraw their children from assembly and RE lessons, but most parents are naturally reluctant to make their children feel out of the ordinary. Besides, they might miss some of the announcements made at assembly. And older children who do not believe in God still have to take part in the worship unless they can persuade their parents to withdraw them. Humanists think it should require a positive decision to join an act of religious worship, not someone else's signature to release you from it – opting in, not opting out.

Many teachers who take collective worship and RE are not really believers themselves, and sometimes they feel coerced into hypocrisy. Needless to say, this worries many religious people as well as humanists. But so far they have been unsuccessful in getting the law changed, despite the number of people against it.

One argument put forward in favour of keeping religion in schools is that without first-hand experience of religion you cannot understand what it means. But, as someone who hated team-games at school, I got some understanding of the joy that ball-game players can experience, not by my own forced participation but by seeing others enjoy themselves in this way – seeing the excitement in their faces and hearing their breathless shouts. So why not just show children films of religious practices, without expecting them to take part in them?

Some Christians have suggested, half-jokingly, that humanists ought to be glad that so many children are put off religion altogether by having it drummed into them at school. But humanists are not glad about it. It can have an anti-educational effect if children are presented with questionable ideas as though they were as uncontroversial as the shape of Australia or an arithmetic answer. What is more, because morality is falsely associated with religion, they may even start behaving badly when they give up religion.

So humanists are always campaigning for the religious clauses of the Education Acts to be repealed. Religion should be left to the home and the chosen place of worship. Humanists are agreeable to children learning in school *about* various religions (not just one), together with the religious legends, provided these are presented *as* legends. Also (and far more important) to their being given moral teaching that does not tie morality up with religious beliefs. Humanists would not want children to be taught even humanist ideas alone, as though they were held by everyone.

Favouring social integration, not sectarian division, humanists are also strongly opposed to denominational (faith) schools, Every child should have a basic right to be part of the common community and to meet with ideas at variance with those at home.

Religious broadcasting

Humanists in Britain complain about the unfair amount of time that is given to Christianity on radio and television, out of all proportion to the number of committed Christians in the country. It is as though almost all the sports time were devoted to one particular sport. The humanist viewpoint rarely gets a hearing, except as part of a religious discussion, to liven it up a bit – and you always know there will be a Christian spokesman standing by to have the last word.

What humanists would like is for every responsible viewpoint on every subject of social controversy to have its fair say, so that everyone can have access to the knowledge necessary to make up their own minds. The pursuit of truth through a free exchange of views is the most important feature of the ideal known as 'the open society'. We can no longer all meet together, as the citizens of ancient Athens did, so radio and television are vital media of communication.

Is humanism a faith?

Humanists do not have a mystic faith, in the sense of believing things on insufficient evidence, but they certainly have faith in human potential.

Because they believe this life is the only life they will have, it is all the more important to humanists to live it to the full, and to provide the best possible conditions of life for people the world over. They put people first. That is what the word humanism means. And they put other animals and the environment – not possessions – second, for the animals share our faculty of feeling and suffering, and all life forms and the environment are inter-dependent.

Because they believe there is no God to turn to, no power to rely on except human powers, humanists stress the importance of self-reliance, human co-operation, and plans based on scientific knowledge. Unlike religious people, who may make some of their decisions according to what the Bible says (or

Humanists are concerned about the quality of life of all human beings around the world

the Qur'an, or other sacred writings) or what their church teaches, humanists can only rely, in the last resort, on their own judgment based on probabilities indicated by the scientific method.

To those who are used to being offered the ready-cooked meals of religious faith, humanism may seem to offer nothing at all. But it points to the ingredients for making your own meal to your own taste, whether alone or in company with others; and it helps clear a space for you to cook it in.

Superstition

Humanism opposes all forms of superstition, not just religious beliefs. Many people today seem to be interested in a mishmash of the so-called paranormal, and beliefs generally known as New Age – though some of these go back to ancient times and are not 'new'.

Some of these beliefs are tied up with Christianity (for instance, miracles, faith-healing, answers to prayer, stigmata, demonic possession); some are tied up with Eastern religions (such as reincarnation, either between species or only within our own species); others (astrology, ghosts, and lucky charms) are even older than world religions themselves, and are often denounced by religious leaders – though many people somehow hold several incompatible sets of belief at the same time. Human beings have

44

latent mental powers of which they are largely unaware, and this can explain some cases of faith-healing and other strange phenomena. But most of the 'psychic' phenomena turn out on investigation to be conjuring tricks, or misremembering, or lies. Besides, ordinary coincidence is much more likely than you might think.

Some superstitions (witchcraft, flying saucers, crop-circles, the Loch Ness monster) are just exaggerated stories; others (apparitions, alien visitations from outer space) may be hallucinations; some (table-rapping, poltergeists, spoon-bending, mind-reading) are conjuring tricks; others (clairvoyance, numerology, materialisation) are confidence tricks. Because most newspapers give space to astrology, people assume there must be something in it, but it is sheer superstition. It is based on the constellations, which are no more than random patterns of stars if viewed from the earth, and there is no possible causal connection between them and human lives.

Fortune-telling devices (horoscopes, ouija boards, tarot cards, palmistry) are often claimed to be just a bit of fun, but vulnerable people can come to believe in them, laying themselves open to exploitation by the 'psychics' and allowing their lives to be ruled by one or more of these superstitions.

Not one of them is true; but reality is far more amazing than all of them put together.

George Bernard Shaw, in his book *The Adventures of the Black Girl in Her Search for God* wrote: 'I am often appalled at the avidity and credulity with which new ideas are snatched at and adopted without a scrap of sound evidence. People will believe anything that amuses them, gratifies them, or promises them some sort of profit.'

Chapter Four: Values – good and bad

'WHAT I cannot understand about you humanists,' a clergyman said to me one day, 'is how you can go through life refusing to believe in the existence of good and evil.' 'We believe, of course, in better and worse,' I replied, 'but I suppose you mean God and the devil: absolute good, and absolute evil.' 'You cannot have comparatives without absolutes' was his parting shot. Why not? Ten miles is longer than nine miles – but is there an absolute longest?

What is conscience?

The idea of absolute perfection, against which everything else must be measured, is part and parcel of the whole religious concept of some other reality behind the reality we experience – a concept which Christianity took over from Platonic philosophy. According to this idea, all the goodness, beauty and truth in this world are reflections of Goodness, Beauty and Truth (the magic of capital letters!) in another, ideal world, which Christians call heaven, and whence, they say, all human values derive. Humanism, on the other hand, recognises no values for human beings to live by that are not derived from human experience.

But we are left with the philosophical problem of how we judge that one thing is better than another. Is it no more than a matter of taste? Bertrand Russell, after a lifetime immersed in philosophy, was still, in his late eighties, looking for a solution to this problem: 'I find myself incapable of believing,' he said, 'that all that is wrong with wanton cruelty is that I don't like it.' However, philosophers (even humanist philosophers) tend to make extraordinarily heavy weather of quite simple matters. To most of us it is self-evident that it is better for sentient beings to experience pleasure and happiness than pain and misery, and that kindness is therefore good and cruelty is bad. If the philosophers persist in asking *how* we know that pleasure and happiness are better than pain and misery, we can only answer that we know it in our bones. Biologically, the desire to avoid pain and misery evolved as important survival factors, and we are the product of our evolutionary past. The animal desire inbred in us to avoid pain and misery, and to help our own kind to avoid them, reach a high point in human sensibility, and it is this sensibility that gives us our moral and aesthetic values.

For an objective theory of ethics you should look to psychology and sociology rather than abstract philosophy, and see how the human being develops a sensibility and conscience through the social conditioning of early childhood. Small children are very selfish; then they go through a legalistic, authoritarian stage. Finally, if they come from a loving home, they achieve moral maturity, with a moral code that is utilitarian and reciprocal. If they offend against their own moral code, they feel uncomfortable. And that is what is meant by 'conscience'. There is nothing mystic about it.

Human values

Some religionists protest that this natural explanation dodges the philosophical difficulty, and that belief in God provides external justification for moral (and other) values. But in fact their philosophical argument just goes round and round, like a dog chasing its tail. We know what we ought to do, they say, by finding out what God commands us to do, for whatever God commands must be right. But to say that God's commands are always right requires some way of judging their rightness apart from the mere fact that God commands them; to say that God is good requires some criterion of goodness apart from the assertion that goodness comes from God. Otherwise such statements are meaningless. This was famously pointed out by Socrates, more than 24 centuries ago, when he asked a pious opponent 'Is it right because the gods approve it, or do they approve it because it is right?' And this brings the argument back where it started: what criteria can there be other than human values? And what is the basis of those values?

Besides, unless we submit God's alleged commands to some sort of human evaluation, how can we be sure that they are in the final interest of human beings? Might not the supposed god be using his human creatures rather as a vivisectionist uses the animals in his laboratory? (See p.76.) If such animals were able to understand their situation, they would surely be justified in hating the vivisectionist; and if they had the power to thwart his intentions, they would surely have every right to do so. But in fact such a god would not even have the excuse of the vivisectionist, who at least thinks he is acting for the good of human beings, whereas a divine tormentor could have no motive apart from sadism.

There is also a practical difficulty in the assertion that in order to know what is right we must find out what God commands – the practical difficulty of recognising the genuine messengers of the divine will, when there are so many rival claimants to the true revelation.

All in all, human reason (fallible though it is), if inspired by human sensibility (however corruptible it may be), is a more reliable moral guide than religious dogma.

The problem of 'evil'

Life is a mixture of good and bad, distributed most unfairly. Some people have more of the good and some have more of the bad – and, of course, this unfairness is something that all decent people deplore and try to do something about. Christians have the consolation of believing that all the injustice in this life will be put right in the next, but humanists, of course, have no such consolation. All they can do is insist on the responsibility of the more fortunate people to help the less fortunate. (That is what humanism is mainly about – but it belongs to the next two chapters rather than this one.)

Since the humanist sees good or bad fortune largely as a matter of impersonal chance, he has no philosophical problem of suffering to contend with – only practical problems of how to minimise

48

disease and other evils. However, to the believer in a personal creator who is both beneficent and all-powerful, misfortune represents a very obstinate philosophical problem, known as 'the problem of evil'. There are several Christian answers to it; they are mostly incompatible, and none of them really provides a solution.

One of the answers is that everything bad in the world is due to the devil – yet the devil, of course, is supposed to be part of God's creation. Another answer is that everything bad is the result of the fall of Adam and Eve – yet we know from the fossil record that animals suffered long before human beings had even evolved. Besides, if the supposed creator had perfect foreknowledge, why did he create an angel with the propensity to turn into Satan, destined to mess up his plans?

We are also told either that people afflicted with misfortune are being punished for offending against God, or, on the other hand (according to Paul's Epistle to the Hebrews), that 'whom the Lord loveth he chasteneth'.

Nature and art

For all its terrible cruelty, nature appeals strongly to the human sense of beauty, and humanists especially turn to nature and art for the sort of satisfaction that religious people can find also in religion. It was a humanist poet, W S Landor, who wrote the famous lines

Nature I loved and, next to Nature, Art;

I warmed both hands before the fire of life;

It sinks, and I am ready to depart.

It is a mistake to think that when we say humanism is based on the scientific method this means that the humanist has no use for music, the visual arts, literature, and the beauties of nature. Indeed, his full-blooded and whole-hearted acceptance of the world makes him all the more appreciative of beauty, which is one of the most important factors that make our lives worth living. And maybe the sad fact that nothing of beauty can last for ever makes beautiful things seem all the more beautiful.

Late comers

In the nineteenth century, when most people in this country still went to church twice on Sundays, the secular societies and ethical societies (which were the forerunners of the humanist groups of today) began to provide for their members the alternative of Sunday evening concerts of secular music – a very daring thing to do in those days. The South Place Ethical Society, which now owns Conway Hall in London, began a series of Sunday evening concerts of chamber-music in 1887, and the series is still going strong today. Said to be the longest series of concerts anywhere in the world, it provides music of the highest standard at very low prices.

A drawing from the 1890s of South Place concert-goers of the day – the original title rebuking them for their late arrival!

Inspiration

Some people say that since the greatest music ever written was church music and the greatest works of painting and sculpture were of religious subjects, the most potent inspiration of the arts must be religion. But this is not so. Unlike that of the ancient Greeks and the Arabs, the music of the Christian Middle Ages was very inferior, and it was not until the eighteenth century that its great modern development began. Then much of the best church music was composed by men who were apostates from Christianity to humanism. Beethoven, for instance, rejected religion, though he wrote some of the greatest religious compositions of all time.

50

(When a friend jokingly wrote on one of his manuscripts the words 'With God's help', Beethoven altered it to 'Man, help thyself.') But the Church was the richest employer of musicians and artists for hundreds of years, so the musicians composed Masses and the artists painted religious pictures in order to earn a living. Their secular works, however, were of the same high quality.

The wealth of the Church was even more exclusive in the sphere of architecture, as the sublime cathedrals of the Middle Ages bear witness. (Unfortunately, most modern church buildings are far less beautiful!) Ironically enough, humanists are usually among the most ardent preservationists of beautiful churches, though they have no say in the use to which they are put, in spite of the fact that their ancestors, like everyone else's, had to pay (through compulsory tithes, for example) for them to be built. But they regard them as part of our great human heritage of man-made beauty. Just as one can feel reverent awe in the Parthenon without believing in the Greek goddess Athene in whose honour it was built, so one can have similar feelings in Canterbury Cathedral or York Minster without believing in God or Jesus Christ.

As for the beauties of nature, you certainly don't need me to say what delight you can get from a range of mountains, a sunset, or a butterfly wing.

Scenes of natural beauty have inspired many non-religious artists and composers

Chapter Five: Morals – right and wrong

*T*HE humanist view of morality is that it is simply practical codes of human conduct, devised by human beings for human benefit.

'It's all very well,' perhaps you are saying, 'but if humanists have no belief in God or a hereafter, why bother to live decent lives? Why not just get whatever they can out of life and let everyone else go hang?'

This line of argument implies that religious people need to be bribed with promises of reward, like naughty children, before they can be expected to behave decently towards their neighbour. But I have a higher opinion than that of people's innate decency – of most people's, anyway. If people live good lives only because of the promise of heaven or threat of hell, is that what most of us mean by 'good'? A child might do what it is told in order to get a lollipop, but is it really a good child? If it behaves well in order to be liked by other people, that also is self-interest, but a higher kind of self-interest, independent of the uncertain supply of lollipops.

Even lower animals (including social insects, such as ants) have co-operative instincts as well as selfish ones, and the survival of a species often depends on a strong co-operative instinct. So it is a part of our evolutionary heritage; and the fact is that you cannot really enjoy life if you are treating your neighbour in a way that offends your natural human feelings and the social conditioning of your early childhood.

In our modern civilisation, with news travelling instantaneously around the globe, everybody has become your neighbour; and, unless you are lacking in imagination, you will feel sympathy for people involved in disaster, even in a country you know little about. Doing something to make someone else happier, especially someone close to you but even someone you can only imagine, generally makes you feel happier yourself.

Freewill and determinism

Determinism means that every event (including every human action) in the universe is caused by prior events. The alternative to determinism is indeterminism or randomness. If uncaused events affected the brain, responsible action would be impossible. Believers in a good and almighty god generally believe in human freedom of will – for how, otherwise, could their god blame human beings for their 'sins', let alone for all the suffering in the world?

Most humanists, however, insofar as the old 'freewill versus determinism' argument lingers on, are determinists. This is not to deny that we do make choices, but it means that we are less free than we feel we are, since our decisions are determined (caused) by the genes we were born with (heredity) and the things that have happened to us during our lives (environment) – for what else is there to cause them? This realisation tends to make secular humanists more understanding of people's behaviour.

The interaction of genes and experience of life determines one's desires, moral fibre, sensitivity, strength of will, intellectual integrity, and so on. Gaining a sense of moral responsibility depends largely on the way one is brought up, modified by later influences and repetitions of behaviour patterns. These facets of one's character then become determining factors themselves, affecting one's actions, and being in turn affected by them. So it is well worth cultivating good habits! But it is unfair to blame people and punish them for what they are, though society certainly needs protection against anti-social actions. The eighteenth-century philosophers David Hume and Immanuel Kant represented determinism and freewill respectively, as the following verse of mine explains:-

> Opposing Hume's deterministic view,
> Freewill for humankind did Kant infer
> To justify God's ire when people err.
> Which view is true? Has Hume or Kant won through?
> While we may choose to do what we prefer,
> We cannot choose what we prefer to do.

53

Moral rules

Apart from having regard for the wild life, there would be no need for any moral rules if you were living alone on a desert island, like Robinson Crusoe. But as soon as Man Friday came along, a reciprocal rule against cannibalism would be necessary if the two inhabitants of the island were to sleep easy.

In society at large, rules have been codified as law, but humanists do not think personal morality is a proper target for the law unless one's immoral actions

The Bible says Moses carried the Ten Commandments down the mountain on two stone tablets

cause suffering. The moral and legal codes of human communities, such as the Judeo-Christian Ten Commandments, may contain particular rules that seem a bit pointless, and even religious people sometimes fail to keep the less useful ones ('Remember the Sabbath day to keep it holy') or even the socially important ones ('Thou shalt not steal'). So what about humanists? They do not, of course, subscribe to a written moral code like the Ten Commandments, but they would generally agree with perhaps six of the ten (from number five onwards), subject to reservations for special circumstances.

This broad agreement is no accident, for all moral codes, even those which are said to derive from divine revelation, were designed in the first place for social utility: that is, on the 'utilitarian' principle mentioned in chapter 2. This is not always recognised by later generations trying to live by the moral code, especially if the code is said to be god-given, but those who first laid down the rules (and the supernatural sanctions) were certainly motivated by social (including selfish) utility.

54

The first four of the Ten Commandments were socially useful to those who were trying to weld a number of wandering tribes into a nation, but they are less useful today. That is the worst thing about hard-and-fast rules that are put into sacred books: they cannot be amended to suit changing circumstances. So, although all moral codes begin with a utilitarian basis, religions tend to ossify them, whereas humanism retains the utilitarian principle that keeps the rule relevant.

Utilitarianism

Basically, what the doctrine of utilitarianism says is that the rightness of actions is to be judged by their consequences. This involves a value-judgment, and the utilitarians of the early nineteenth century maintained that what was right was that which promoted 'the greatest happiness of the greatest number'. As a rough guide this is a good principle, but its statistical element might conceivably rob an individual, or a small minority, of the basic conditions necessary to make life worth living at all; and in such a case humanists would put the fundamental happiness of the individual or minority before the superficial happiness of everybody else; for the chief principle of humanism is that every human being is an end in himself or herself, and may never be wholly exploited as a means to an end. It makes sense for those who believe in a life hereafter to sacrifice individual lives, or urge individuals to sacrifice their own lives, in the interests of others, since they believe that the individual will reap a due reward after death; but the humanist has no such justification. The only person who can decide what purposes would be worth sacrificing his life for is, on humanist principles, that person himself.

The Golden Rule

'Do as you would be done by.' That is good, reciprocal, utilitarian morality. There are two versions of it in the Bible: 'Thou shalt love thy neighbour as thyself' (which Jesus quoted from Leviticus), and 'Whatsoever ye would that men should do unto you, do ye even so to them.' Other versions of the same advice occur in ancient China (Confucius and Lao-tse), ancient Greece and Rome, and most other civilisations. It is called the Golden Rule.

But Bernard Shaw wrote: 'Do not do unto others as you would that they should do unto you. Their tastes may not be the same.' It is clear enough what he was getting at, and whom he was getting at: the busybody 'do-gooders' who think they know far better than we do what is good for us. Nevertheless, if due allowance is made for differences of taste, the golden rule is an excellent guide in the maze of moral dilemmas. And it has its golden feet very firmly on humanist ground, not religious ground – for, whether or not it is given in holy books, it is based on utilitarianism, not on any special revelation, specific commandments, or sacred taboos.

Shaw goes on to say: 'The golden rule is that there are no golden rules.' In other words, there is no rule so golden as to be sacrosanct. This warning, however, is also very much in the humanist tradition – the tradition of rejecting absolutes, judging every case on its merits, and, above all, treating each individual as an individual. Therefore, as Shaw suggests, the rule should be applied with an open mind and with imaginative respect for minority and personal differences, whether of taste, custom, or sheer cussedness. That said, the golden rule remains the soundest moral principle there is – not only as a guide to our individual actions but also as a means of justifying one's actions to others, and as an assurance of reciprocity.

It is sometimes suggested that negative versions of the golden rule are more reliable than the positive ones, and perfectly adequate. Examples of negative versions are: 'What thou thyself hatest do to no man' (Tobit), and 'What you would avoid suffering yourself seek not to impose upon others' (the Stoic slave and teacher, Epictetus). And this form of the rule is certainly less susceptible to Shaw's objection.

Future generations

The golden rule can also be applied to unborn generations, and humanism is deeply concerned with the responsibility of each succeeding generation to bequeath to the future a world as good to live in as possible. After all, while religious people may look to a life hereafter, the only future life for humanists is that of future generations.

It is not surprising, therefore, that humanists are strongly represented in the pressure groups concerned with over-population, pollution, conservation, predicted climate changes, and other aspects of ecology. (For instance, it was a member of the British humanist movement who started the Conservation Society in the 1950s.)

The population 'explosion'

Year (CE)

Since the second World War most educated people have become aware of the threat of ever-increasing human numbers, known as 'the population explosion' – or, rather, it has become too apparent for people to close their eyes to it any longer. The world population explosion started about 1650, and the British population explosion about a hundred years later. The theory of population growth outstripping food supplies was first worked out by an English economist, T R Malthus (1766-1834), who advocated cutting down the birth rate by raising the age of marriage!

Towards the end of the nineteenth century, many freethinkers, seeing the need for limiting the population but realising the

57

impracticality of advocating later marriage, began advocating contraception instead. They were called neo-Malthusians. One of them, Charles Bradlaugh (who was also an important parliamentarian, writer, editor, and reformer, and founder of the National Secular Society) was, in 1877, together with his friend Annie Besant, sentenced to six months' imprisonment plus a £200 fine each (though the convictions were later quashed, on a technicality) for publishing a pamphlet about family planning. People were not allowed to know that it was possible for them to limit their families. They were supposed to leave that decision to God. Besides, according to the Bible, God had said 'increase and multiply'. But when that was written, it was necessary to have enough young people coming along to farm the land, and defend it from invasion, and the main danger then was under-population, especially in times of plague. Modern medicine and sanitation changed all that, and the fact that the churches were unprepared to change their teaching to fit in with this, while humanists immediately responded to the new situation, shows that specific commandments are less adaptable than the humanist way of simply putting forward a moral principle on which to base one's decisions.

Since humanists do not accept the idea of life after death for the individual who has died, their hopes are centred on this world and on future generations. So they are particularly concerned about environmental issues. At the same time, they want environmental issues to be kept in balance: for instance, the rich countries, which cause most of the pollution of the planet and the wastage of its natural resources, should not use environmental arguments to stifle economic development in the poorer countries where more intermediate technology and better distribution of food and medicine are the first requirements. But humanists advocate family planning throughout the world, since continued population growth is at the root of most environmental, health, resource, and migration problems.

Sexual morality

Sexual morality is just one facet of general morality, not a special case. Humanists are not among those who condemn all sexual activity outside marriage. Rather, they see sex as one of the great pleasures of life, not just the means of reproduction. But sex is something one has to be even more careful about than crossing the road.

In the sexual field, as in everything else, the general humanist moral principle applies: as long as you are not harming or imposing your will on anyone else, what you do is your own business.

But it is certainly very immoral to risk conceiving a baby that you do not want and cannot look after, for that possible baby is your responsibility. And there are more than enough babies in the world without having any that are not really wanted, whether inside or outside marriage.

To risk spreading disease from one person to another is also, of course, most immoral. So is playing fast-and-loose with anyone's affections: you cannot always avoid hurting people's feelings, but you should always try to avoid it. Consideration (which is application of the Golden Rule) is one of the most important human qualities, and nowhere more important than in sexual relationships.

What is the humanist attitude to homosexuality? Unlike most religions (including mainstream Christianity, Orthodox Judaism and Islam), which generally condemn gay sex in line with the teachings in their ancient 'holy' books, modern humanism recognises that, for some people, same-sex attraction is a fact of life and that the way in which individuals express their sexuality is a matter for them alone, provided they are not harming or exploiting others.

About five in every hundred people are primarily homosexual, yet male homosexuality was against the law in this country until 1967, and many people were sent to prison for homosexual activity, which has existed throughout history. People we now call 'gay' include the Roman Emperor Hadrian, the renaissance sculptor

Michelangelo, the Victorian playwright Oscar Wilde, the computer pioneer and WW2 code-breaker Alan Turing, the present-day actor Sir Ian McKellen, and the rock star Sir Elton John. The Ancient Greek poet Sappho, who wrote love poems to another woman, lived in a community of women on the island of Lesbos, which is why we call gay women 'lesbians'. Gays are found in all walks of life and make as valuable a contribution to society as their heterosexual counterparts; but they still face a great deal of prejudice and have yet to achieve complete legal equality. The Gay and Lesbian Humanist Association (GALHA) together with its associated educational charity, the Pink Triangle Trust, explain that homophobia (the fear and hatred of homosexuals) is a social evil, similar to racism. One of the activities of the PTT is to provide officiants for gay and lesbian 'weddings' or affirmation ceremonies, as a secular alternative to the gay 'blessing' offered by some of the more progressive churches.

Abortion

Abortion is another controversial issue. It is a mistake to say that humanists are in favour of abortion: no one can be happy about the need for abortion, which, except in unforeseen circumstances, is the result of failed contraception. But humanists do regard abortion as better than bringing unwanted babies into the world. In 1936, a group of women, who had been doing pioneering work in the family-planning clinics that were beginning to open in the big towns, set up the Abortion Law Reform Association, because they had seen the terrible results of 'backstreet' abortions to which women resorted for lack of legal abortion. But their Association remained small until 1962, when the thalidomide disaster aroused public demand for abortion to be made legal. Then, with the support of the humanist movement together with some individuals who were not humanists, the Abortion Law Reform Association became much stronger and very active, resulting in the passing of the Abortion Act of 1967. This has enabled thousands of women to have abortions carried out properly in hospital, instead of risking dangerous amateur abortions or having babies to whom they could not give proper care. But the chances of getting a legal abortion still depend on the personal views of one's doctor, so the campaign now is for early abortion on request, as well as having to fight persistent fundamentalist attempts to ban all later abortions, however crucial.

Marriage and divorce

Most young adults choose to set up house with one other person of the opposite sex. This is also a very convenient way of bringing up any children they may have. It is usual for the couple to get married – marriage being a social contract to give the partnership stability, mutual insurance, economic security, and recognition by society. But there are some disadvantages in marriage, especially if the partners ever want to dissolve the partnership.

Until 1971, divorce was allowed under English law if only one of the partners wanted it, but not if they both agreed about it! Many people, including all humanists, thought this the very opposite of common sense, so the Divorce Reform Act 1969 was passed, and the courts now recognise one reason only for granting divorce: the irreparable breakdown of the marriage.

Most humanists who want to start a family get married, but some prefer to trust each other without legal marriage. It has even been suggested that living together and having children without the bondage of marriage makes for a stronger bond, and if one or both of the partners want to make love with some new partner there is less pressure to break the first partnership in order to do so.

Those humanists who choose to get married almost always have a register-office wedding. But some of them also like to have a special non-religious wedding ceremony at a larger gathering of their friends and relations. After all, ritual is an important part of culture, and it does not have to be religious ritual. For instance, shaking hands and blowing out the candles on a birthday-cake are common non-religious rituals. There is now an extensive panel of humanist officiants, who are able to lead non-religious weddings, gay affirmation ceremonies, baby-namings, and funerals. Some humanists think there should be more humanist ritual of this kind, but others think it more important to try to get the public facilities improved for the benefit of everybody, whether humanists or not – for instance, to provide larger and more elegant register offices for weddings, to make them available in the evening – a popular time for weddings – and to make the legal ceremonial more flexible.

Freedom of action

Adults have a duty to protect the young from doing harm to themselves before they are old enough to understand the consequences of their actions – to protect toddlers from walking into the fire; six-year-olds from crossing a busy road; twelve-year-olds from starting the smoking habit; and fifteen-year-olds from conceiving babies or contracting venereal disease. But once you become adult you become a member of the responsible generation, and humanists do not believe that anyone has the right to take that responsibility from you. Every adult human being of sound mind should have, in the words of John Stuart Mill, 'perfect freedom, legal and social, to do the action and stand the consequences' – provided, of course, one is not thereby infringeing the freedom of others. Only by freely choosing what to make of our lives can we attain our full stature and human dignity.

Humanists, therefore, do not agree with censorship, at least for adults. By what right can anyone presume to decide what other people shall be allowed to see or read? Every member of the responsible generation has the right to choose such things for himself or herself.

This does not mean that humanists approve of everything that is printed, filmed, shown on the stage or television or posted on the internet, but they say it is up to each individual to decide what he or she shall see or read. At the same time, they uphold your freedom not to have things thrust upon you that you might want to avoid, so

62

items that might offend some people ought to be kept out of public sight, as long as they are freely obtainable by anyone who asks for them, and as long as it is generally known that they are obtainable.

Not only is censorship unjustifiable in itself, but once it creeps in it begins to slow down cultural progress, for things that are considered to be in bad taste often include new ideas of real value.

It is most important that the general public should have all possible information relevant to making up their minds how to act. But if plenty of warning has been given about, say, the grave health risk in heavy smoking, and people still choose to take that risk, then, on humanist principles, no one has a right to stop them from doing so, though one certainly has the right to try to dissuade them.

On the other hand, it is not really fair that people should be tempted by clever advertisements to do things (such as smoking) that are against their long-term interests. So there is a case for curbing such advertisements, which are thrust upon the public unasked for (with the object of making more money for shareholders), even at the risk of causing illness and early death. One of the most useful things you can learn in the modern world is to be wary of the temptations of advertisers. And you should realise how foolish it is to take any drugs just for kicks or to look big, whether drugs that are illegal, such as cannabis at present, or those that happen to be legal, such as ordinary cigarettes and alcohol. As for hard drugs, which are physically addictive, to experiment with these is really asking for serious trouble that could ruin the whole chance of a full, happy, exciting life, that you won in that cosmic lottery.

Freedom to die with dignity

Although life is something to be highly prized, certain intolerable conditions – for instance, an incurable disease of a painful or distressing nature – may wipe out all its value. Unlike religious people, most of whom say that the time of death must always be left to God, humanists say there is no purpose in prolonging life beyond the point where it has no more value to the person himself or herself. The humanist sees it as a fundamental human right to be able to choose to die.

Here again it is only comparatively recently that the law of this country has been reformed so as to allow suicide. Until 1961 suicide was illegal – though, of course, it was only unsuccessful suicide attempts that offenders could be punished for! (Except, that is, for the 'punishment' of not being given a Christian funeral.)

It is still against the law to help someone else to commit suicide – and, indeed, it is obvious why this should be so. However, humanists think that one kind of suicide help should be allowed – and that is the kind known as voluntary 'euthanasia' (easy death), in the case of incurable illness. (Incurable, that is, at the time of decision, and unlikely to become curable during the expected course of the disease.)

Most humanists support Dignity in Dying (formerly the Voluntary Euthanasia Society), which advocates the legalisation of a procedure by which healthy adults could sign a document to say that if they should fall victim to incurable illness or injury of a serious and distressing nature they wish to be given a lethal injection. It would then be up to the doctors in charge of the case to decide when that point had been reached, though the consent of the patient would probably be required again, together with that of close relatives and an independent doctor. But there is a great deal of opposition to this proposal, even though it would affect only those people who were in favour of it.

Potential human beings

Another type of euthanasia which some (but not all) humanists would like made legal is euthanasia for seriously defective newborn babies – and this, of course, could not be voluntary. People who are opposed to it say (if they believe in God) that only God has the right to decide whether a baby, however seriously handicapped, should live or die, and also (whether they believe in God or not) that no

64

one has the right to take any human life but their own, except at that person's free request. People on the other side of the argument say that no one has the right to condemn someone else to live when the chances of a worthwhile life are so low. Also, in most cases the parents could produce a perfectly healthy baby in a year's time – and since we now have a social duty to limit our families it is only sensible to limit them to those who have a reasonable chance of a happy life. Besides, at the moment of birth a baby is really only a potential human being, for one becomes fully human only through relating to other people. Once a baby gets to know its mother, and the family get to know the baby, it becomes a person, and then it is too late to make such a decision. Any living children with defects, whether congenital or otherwise, should, of course, be given every possible assistance to fulfil their capabilities.

Another social issue on which humanists differ from many religious believers is that of human embryology – embryo research, genetic engineering, the use of stem-cells (which can develop into different cells for patients with various defects) for research or surgical implants, the cloning of human organs, and so on. Humanists say an embryo has no rights until it develops a functional nervous system and is capable of feeling pain. Whether they are fertilised or not, eggs are not people.

Believers often insist that it is immoral to interfere with nature – though in fact they themselves are interfering with nature whenever they accept medical or surgical treatment!

Chapter Six: Living as a humanist

*T*HE fact that so far this book has dealt mainly with abstract ideas may have given you the impression that humanism is only for intellectuals. If so, it is a false impression. After all, you would get a similar impression about Christianity from reading a work of theology. And humanism is for living. In fact, living is what it is all about.

Sometimes, when people hear about humanism for the first time, they say, 'Well, I've been a humanist all my life, and didn't know it!' And a schoolgirl once asked me: 'Why do they have to call it an ism? It's just plain common sense!' But, of course, not everyone agrees with it; though even the traditional religions are becoming more and more humanistic year by year.

Organised humanism

Because humanism has an independent sort of outlook, most humanists see no reason to join a humanist organisation. This has the unfortunate result that the membership of the various humanist organisations is only a fraction of the numerical strength of humanism in the population at large, and some people measure its right to have a say in affairs by the number of paid-up members the organisations have, instead of by the number of people who agree with them.

But some humanists do realise the importance of banding together, in order to establish the legitimacy of their views, so that they can profess them with confidence and without injury to their children; also in order to be able to help each other make decisions — for the personal responsibility that humanism entails is too difficult for most people to cope with on their own and it eases the burden to work things out with others who share one's basic assumptions.

In Britain there are three national humanist organisations

(British Humanist Association, National Secular Society, and Rationalist Association). There is a London-based humanist society (South Place Ethical Society) owning the Conway Hall Humanist Centre. There are regional organisations in Scotland, Wales and the north of Ireland, and many small local humanist groups. The main reasons for there being so many different bodies are historical; but they each retain their own particular emphasis, though they also work together on particular projects and have a considerable overlap in their membership.

Many distinguished philosophers, scientists, artists, writers, and entertainers are associated with the humanist movement.

Comic actor and writer, Stephen Fry, is a humanist. There's plenty of room in humanism for laughter and enjoyment of life, as well as more serious concerns

Each of the major humanist organisations has a magazine. The Rationalist Association publishes *New Humanist;* the British Humanist Association has its *BHA News;* and South Place Ethical Society, the *Ethical Record;* while *The Freethinker,* founded in 1881, is associated with the National Secular Society, which also has its own *Bulletin.*

The British Humanist Association (founded 1963) absorbed the Ethical Union (founded 1896). Also from the nineteenth century are the National Secular Society (1866) and Rationalist Press Association (1899) while Leicester Secular Society, with its Secular Hall, survives from the 1850s.

South Place Ethical Society is oldest of all (founded 1793), though it has gone through several changes of name, having evolved from a congregation of Christian dissenters who rejected the prevailing doctrine of hell, through unitarianism, to a modern humanist position. Among their speakers in the past century are many famous names, including Felix Adler, A J Ayer, Annie Besant, Colin Blakemore, Alex Comfort, Richard Dawkins, A C Grayling, Laurence Housman, Julian Huxley, T H Huxley, Neil Kinnock, Margaret Knight, Prince Kropotkin, William Morris, Gilbert Murray, Bertrand Russell, Bernard Shaw, Leslie Stephen, Sidney Webb, Rebecca West, Barbara Wootton and Israel Zangwill.

The National Secular Society also has a very interesting history. Its founder, Charles Bradlaugh, was involved not only in the criminal conviction already mentioned, for publishing a pamphlet on family planning, but also in a large number of other court actions, several of which established important principles of civil liberty. In 1880 he was elected as

Cartoon from a contemporary magazine of Charles Bradlaugh (1833-1891) pictures him as a stubborn elephant, difficult to remove from Parliament

Member of Parliament for Northampton, but his request to substitute secular affirmation for the usual religious oath taken by MPs on entering Parliament was refused, and when he therefore said he would take the oath, he was not allowed to do so because of his known atheism, nor allowed to take his seat without the oath! So the parliamentary seat to which he had been elected was declared vacant, However, each time a by-election was held in Northampton, Bradlaugh was re-elected, and he was finally allowed to enter Parliament in 1886. Two years later he got the law changed so that MPs could choose to substitute a non-religious form of affirmation for the oath, but he died before he had the opportunity to use it himself.

Born in the same year as Bradlaugh, but across the Atlantic, was one of the greatest of American humanists, Robert G Ingersoll, who had similar views to Bradlaugh and waged similar campaigns in the United States. He was a brilliant orator and writer, and his writings still inspire people today. One of his famous sayings is 'The time to be happy is now, the place to be happy is here, and the way to be happy is to make others so.' Another American humanist of the same era was the celebrated author of *Tom Sawyer* and *Huckleberry Finn*, who wrote under the name Mark Twain (1835-1910).

'Blasphemy'

The first editor of *The Freethinker,* G W Foote (1850-1915), was sent to prison for a year in 1883 for the crime of 'blasphemy'. Bradlaugh tried in vain to get the Blasphemy Laws repealed, but it took until May 2008 for the criminal offence of blasphemy to be abolished. The last time anyone was imprisoned for blasphemy here was in 1922, when J W Gott was cruelly sentenced to nine months' imprisonment with hard labour, which caused his early death, but as late as 1977, *Gay News* and its editor were fined heavily for blasphemy.

In addition to the campaign against the blasphemy laws and to all the political and social campaigns mentioned in Chapter 5, the humanist movement has fought consistently for women's liberation, for prison reform, for the abolition of capital punishment (finally achieved in 1965), for the abolition of corporal punishment in schools and other institutions, for the better treatment of the mentally ill, for the abolition of cruel sports, and for innumerable other social causes, as well as such minor freedoms as Sunday entertainment and Sunday trading, which we now take for granted.

Overseas humanist organisations

Most countries have their own humanist organisations, each of which applies the general humanist principles to their own situation, and their activities vary according to existing laws and customs. But the direction in which all of them are moving is towards the secularisation of society and greater freedom for the individual.

Many of them are federated through the International Humanist and Ethical Union, which was formed in 1952. It now has about 90 member organisations in 35 countries, fosters the growth of humanist groups around the world, and holds World Humanist Congresses every two years. Apart from initiating policies and coordinating the activities of its member groups, IHEU represents the interests of the world-wide humanist movement at the United Nations, at UNICEF (New York) and in the Council of Europe (Strasbourg), where it is recognised as an international NGO with consultative status. It also maintains operational relations with UNESCO in Paris.

In India, particularly, several humanist organisations are engaged in large-scale social reforms. The Indian Radical Humanist Association is active in the all-party democratic movement in the country and helped found Citizens for Democracy and the People's Union of Civil Liberties. Its chairman for more than two decades, Justice V M Tarkunde, was one of India's most respected human-rights activists, while its late president, Dr/Mrs Indumati Parikh, worked for more than thirty years among the slum dwellers of Bombay. She founded an organisation called *Streehitakarini,* to give young women education and status, and to promote family planning. It takes medical assistance to people's homes, gives nutritional advice, tries to dispel commonly held superstitions, and holds training classes for adolescents in good citizenship and humanism.

On the opposite side of India (in Vijayawada) there is another foundation, known as the Atheist Centre, which likewise runs a number of health and social projects. One of these is a school where the children of *devadhasis* – women forced by tradition to become temple prostitutes – are rehabilitated. The Centre has even managed to rescue some of the prostitutes themselves, by arranging marriages for them. It also exposes the god-men's magic tricks and superstitions. Another of its intriguing activities is holding an occasional anti-taboo feast, at which vegetarians will try a small piece of fish or meat, Hindus a morsel of beef, and people from a Muslim background a taste of pork.

Some 200 miles to the south, in Madras, is *Dravidar Kazhagam*, the largest atheist pressure group in the world – and the most influential, both philosophically and politically. Founded in 1944 by a greatly respected social reformer, it is opposed to Brahminism and combats superstition, caste, poverty, and discrimination, and, like *Streehitakarini,* is particularly concerned with the emancipation of women, the remarriage of young widows, and education for the poor.

Ceremonies

The ceremonies provided by some humanist organisations also vary from country to country, according to the expectations of each particular culture. The British do not seem to feel the need for much ritual in their lives, and the only humanist ceremony for which there is very much demand in Britain is the funeral. Most humanists are cremated, and all the British humanist organisations have a network of people who have been trained to lead a funeral, taking the

Nowadays many people choose to have a humanist funeral. Here Barbara Smoker officiates at a humanist funeral at a crematorium

71

place of a minister of religion. A humanist funeral is not about a supposed future life, of course, but celebrates the life which has just come to an end but which will live on in people's memories.

There is also a smaller, but increasing, demand for humanist weddings, gay affirmations (which can now be registered as civil partnerships – equivalent to weddings), and baby-naming ceremonies; while in some other countries there are other humanist ceremonies. In Norway, where it is the custom for almost every adolescent to be confirmed, young people from humanist families would feel they were missing something if they did not have their own growing-up initiation ceremony; so after receiving a course in moral studies, they take part in a 'civil confirmation' ceremony in their humanist group, as a sign that they have become adult. Even in Britain there is a much greater demand for humanist ceremonies today than there was when the first edition of this book came out.

Social action

Humanist organisations do not duplicate social work that is being done well by other bodies. And even if it is not being done well but public resources are there for doing it, they prefer to act as a pressure group to get it done better by the proper agency, than to set up a new charity. As individuals, they tend to do voluntary work through the United Nations agencies, national and local welfare services, and undenominational voluntary bodies with specific aims. But where there is a gap, they try to fill it.

For instance, there used to be a gap in the facilities for the adoption of babies, because most adoption societies were run by religious denominations on a religious basis, so that people of no religion found it almost impossible to adopt babies at all. In addition to pressing for non-denominational adoption facilities to be provided by local councils, the national humanist organisations got together in 1963 to found the Agnostics Adoption Society, which later changed its name to the Independent Adoption Society. It was generally recognised as one of the best-run adoption

72

agencies in the country, and led to reform of the adoption laws.

At the other end of life, there was another need – elderly people needed homes where they could retain their independence yet have companionship and help when required. So the Humanist Housing Association was formed in 1954 to provide flatlets where elderly people could spend their remaining years in modern comfort, with

Rose Bush Court, in Parkhill Road, London – one of the blocks of flatlets built by the Humanist Housing Association for elderly people

their own furniture and possessions, looking after themselves but with a warden on call in case they needed any help, and communal gardens and sitting-rooms for when they wanted company. This has since become a widely accepted pattern for homes for the elderly. The Humanist Housing Association has now merged with the St Pancras Housing Association, but its houses are still named after humanist activists.

Most of the local humanist groups support particular local, national, or international social projects, and a few have set up their own projects for social action.

In Botswana (Africa), a secondary school which specialised in teaching agriculture was started by a few humanists, and British humanists raised the £1,000 necessary to get it started, in association with War on Want. The actual building work was carried out by the students themselves, who even made the bricks for it! Later it was maintained by the Botswana government. Another humanist project was set up in a poor district of Bihar (India) to supply such primary needs as wells and irrigation. Money for this project was raised by the International Humanist and Ethical Union from humanists in all their member countries, and other similar projects followed.

Students building their own school at Swaneng, Botswana, as part of a project started by humanists, in association with War on Want, and later maintained by the Botswana government

Mostly, however, humanists support such organisations as Oxfam, which have more resources for worthwhile schemes. In any case, the humanist emphasis in social work is not so much to give people things and do things for them as to help them to help themselves. What people want, the world over, is the opportunity to work for the fulfilment of their own life's purposes, free from oppression and discrimination. And this is what humanism is about.

Suggestions for further reading

An ordinary encyclopedia will provide articles on most of the 'isms' mentioned in this book. Further information about humanism, including monthly or quarterly periodicals and free pamphlets, can be obtained from any of the main humanist organisations - see their websites below. If you would like to know more about books on ceremonies, ethics and countering religious arguments, you may request a full publications list from the British Humanist Association, 1 Gower Street, London WC1E 6HD.

Other books of interest:

David Attenborough: *Life on Earth* (Collins, 1992)
David Attenborough: *The Living Planet* (Collins, 1992)
Richard Dawkins: *Climbing Mount Improbable* (Penguin, 2006)
Richard Dawkins: *River Out of Eden - a Darwinian View of Life* (Phoenix, 2001)
Foote & Ball: *The Bible Handbook* (NSS, 1988)
Jostein Gaardner: *Sophie's World, a philosophical story* (Phoenix House, 1999)
Jim Herrick: *Humanism: An Introduction* (RA, 2007)
Margaret Knight: *Humanist Anthology* (revised by Jim Herrick, RPA, 1995)
Richard Norman: *On Humanism* (Routledge, 2004)
Bertrand Russell: *Why I am not a Christian* (RPA, 1961)
Leslie Scrase: *Some Ancestors of Humanism: Precursors of Humanism in the Ancient World* (SPES, 1997)
Barbara Smoker: *Freethoughts* (GW Foote, 2002)

Humanist websites

BHA   – British Humanist Association - **www.humanism.org.uk**
CFI   – Center for Inquiry - **www.centerforinquiry.net**
GALHA – Gay and Lesbian Humanist Association - **www.galha.org**
IHEU   – International Humanist and Ethical Union - **www.iheu.org**
           Leicester Secular Society: - **www.leicestersecularsociety.org.uk**
NSS   – National Secular Society - **www.secularism.org.uk**
R(P)A   – Rationalist (Press) Association - **www.rationalist.org.uk**
SPES   – South Place Ethical Society - **www.ethicalsoc.org.uk**

Acknowledgments

The author wishes to thank the following for their help in providing the photographs and drawings which illustrate this book:
Donald Rooum, Glen Gerber, Joyce Harpur, Martin Harris, Lalla Ward, Mansell Collection, Studio Vista books, the BBC, the Museum of the History of Science at Oxford, National Portrait Gallery London, the Shaw Society, and South Place Ethical Society.

The text was revised and enlarged by the author, with generous input by Norman Bacrac, and published by the South Place Ethical Society.

Monkey's Credo

A poem of mine, *Monkey's Credo* – which is, on the face of it, a protest
against vivisection – has an underlying metaphorical meaning that makes
it relevant to this book. The submissive, unreasonably trusting attitude of
Zed (the monkey) towards the human species echoes that of many people
towards their gods.

A lowly rhesus monkey, I...
born to suffer, born to die;
    bred (my mother said) by man,
    as part of some important plan
designed by human mind on high.
And mine is not to reason why.

My master man, whose name is Ted,
gave me (in likeness) my name, Zed.
    Unnerved by needle? Scared of knife?
    when Ted (to whom I owe my life)
has cared for me and kept me fed?
I'll never fear to hear his tread!

A lonely rhesus monkey, I...
I miss my sisters, Ex and Wye;
    but master is my company,
    for here he walks and talks to me.
Albeit monkeys all must die,
he'll reunite us by-and-by.

Yet, faithlessly I sense with dread
my time approaching to be bled.
    What is the purpose of 'research'?
    Would man leave monkey in the lurch?
My mighty master, tender Ted ...
he'll surely raise me from the dead.

Else how could mankind justify
denying monkey sight of sky,
    imprisoning in metal mesh,
    withholding warmth of kindred flesh...?
Ted's just! In Ted I trust for my
reward, when I to schedule die.

MAN IS LOVE

Z

Drawing by Glen Gerber

The Author

BARBARA SMOKER was born into a Roman Catholic family in London in 1923, and had a convent education. As a girl, she was torn between the ambitions of becoming a nun or a writer – in either case for the greater glory of God; but, after overseas wartime service in the Women's Royal Naval Service, she thought and read a lot about religion and the more she thought and read the less she found it possible to believe. At the age of 26 she finally renounced Christianity and became a secular humanist.

She also became active in various social campaigns, including nuclear disarmament, abolition of the death penalty, prison reform, alphabet reform, homelessness, legalisation of abortion, and voluntary euthanasia; and she served on a large number of committees. Since 1970 she has often officiated at non-religious funerals, and later at wedding ceremonies, gay commitments, and baby-namings; and trained other humanists to do so.

From 1971 to 1996 she was President of the National Secular Society. In 1973 she wrote the first edition of this booklet on humanism, for use in secondary schools. From 1981 to 1985 she chaired the Voluntary Euthanasia Society, and she compiled a book on that subject. Her other writings include a book of satirical verse, *Good God!*, and a cassette script, *Atheism on a Soap-Box*, and she wrote a pamphlet against the banning of embryo research, *Eggs Are Not People*, which was sent to all Members of Parliament in 1985. The same year she recorded a radio talk, 'Why I Am an Atheist', for the BBC World Service, and over the years has put her humanist views across in innumerable radio and television programmes, as well as in print, in lectures, and in university debates.

In 1984 she undertook a five weeks' speaking tour of the United States, and in 1990 a similar tour of India. In 1986, a letter she wrote on the dangers of segregating children in different religious schools was signed by 22 distinguished persons and published in *The Guardian* and elsewhere. When Muslim extremists held a march in London on May 27,1989, calling for the death of Salman Rushdie, Barbara Smoker stood on the route with a homemade banner reading 'Free Speech', and survived a physical attack by a surge of demonstrators. In 1998 she visited India again, to inaugurate a mass atheist rally, and in 2002 brought out a collection of her articles called *Freethoughts*.

The International Humanist and Ethical Union honoured her in 2005 with a lifetime achievement award for 'Distinguished Services to Humanism'.

Index